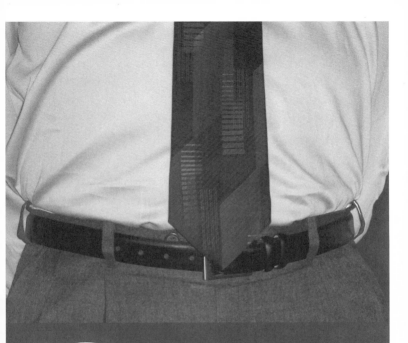

10 Questions
Every Husband Should Ask His Wife Every Year

Tom Elliff
Author of *Letters to Lovers*

Ten Questions

Every Husband Should Ask His Wife Every Year

Published by Living in the Word Publishing

©2004

By Thomas Elliff

Subject Heading: FAMILY LIFE/MARRIAGE

Italics are the author's own emphasis.

Unless otherwise noted, Scripture quotations are from KJV King James Version. Some Scriptures were paraphrased by the author.

Contact information:

Living in the Word Publishing • P.O. Box 891474

Oklahoma City, OK 73189-1474

TABLE OF CONTENTS

This book is dedicated to every husband who has the courage to ask, to listen, and to lovingly respond to his wife. You are truly "dwelling with her according to knowledge…"

(1 Peter 3:7)

AUTHOR'S PREFACE

We live in a culture that accepts marital failure as the norm. In my own home state, almost one-third of the adult population has experienced divorce and the ravaging heartaches associated with it. Over forty percent of our nation's married couples say that they are *not very happy*. And many couples, while not contemplating divorce, still have no answer for the fact that they are at an impasse, not moving forward in their relationship.

This world desperately needs to see some *great marriages*. Like people themselves, great marriages come in all shapes and sizes. But they all have one thing in common...*great communication between a husband and wife*. That's the issue this small book addresses. Great communication involves asking the right questions of your mate and listening for the *heart response*. So read it with your own heart open as well!

A special thanks is due my wife, Jeannie. She is willing for me to ask the hard questions and patient as I seek to understand her answers and respond appropriately. She is the perfect wife in every way. Neal and Jennifer Livingston have assisted enormously in preparing the text of this book. And Mike Hand has capably overseen its publication. Broadman and Holman Publishers are also due my special gratitude. In chapters five and six they have allowed me to quote generously from a book of mine they published in 2003, *Letters to Lovers*. Thank you to Kelton Spears and the staff at Paragon Press who diligently worked to help create this book.

A NOTE TO HUSBANDS

Families are in trouble. Last year, in my own country, an average of almost 3,600 divorces occurred each day of the year. It is impossible to accurately measure the debris left in the trail of those broken homes. There are so many stresses that are passed down from one generation to another. There are stresses of single-parenting, confused ideas regarding moral authority, economic pressures, hopelessness, despair, and the creation of a divorce-culture. These and other negative results of divorce appear like contrails behind a plane—visible long after the actual cause is out of view. Once the rationalizing is over, there is no debating the fact that broken homes leave a lingering trail of broken lives.

In every substantive study of broken marriages, the failure to communicate adequately is listed among the top three causes. (The other two are generally related to moral infidelity or financial pressure, issues which are closely connected to failed communication). Why is this the case? Where does it start? Who is primarily responsible? What can be done about it? These are more than fair questions. They are questions which we must ask and answer if we are to change the culture of divorce which will inevitable destroy our society.

I don't know how you came across this little book. Did someone give it to you? Did you just happen upon it? Did you purchase it out of a desire to strengthen your marriage? Are you contemplating marriage and want to start out right? Did you reach for it as a drowning man would reach out to the hand of a rescuer? I can tell you this—applying the simple tools given to you in these pages can make all the difference in the world! I know this from personal experience and from the multiplied testimonies of those who are now using it.

What is that tool? We'll get to that soon enough! First, I want you to consider what follows on the very next page. As you do, take note of the fact that there are many men who have preceded you in this journey. They know the power of this simple tool! They are praying that God will show you how to use it as well!

One final note. You cannot read this little book without concluding that the author is a believer in Christ. Years ago I trusted in Him as my Savior and seek to daily honor Him as Lord of my life. Now, after over forty years of speaking, teaching, and counseling on family issues, I am convinced *that one decision* makes all the difference in any home. My wife, Jeannie, and I have four children and twenty grandchildren. After thirty-eight years of marriage, we are encouraged that our children also embrace the principles contained in these pages. Our prayer is that you will do the same!

Yours for the home that reveals the heart of God!

Tom Elliff

1

WHAT IF...

✏ You suddenly came across the secret for opening the heart of your wife—an incredible ability to really see her greatest desires, fears, frustrations, dreams, and aspirations?

✏ You had the ability to hear something other than mere words as your wife spoke to you—the ability to hear the deep longings of her heart?

✏ You and your wife could live the balance of your lives together in genuine harmony; you had a plan for resolving conflict that enabled the entire family to be the "winner"?

∽ You had the ability to invite your wife into your own heart, so that she knew your greatest desires and goals, felt free to ask you questions about them, and knew how to join you in achieving them?

∽ You could rest at the end of each day with the confidence you had obeyed the scriptural admonition to "dwell with your wife according to wisdom?"

∽ You could overcome a major obstacle to answered prayer; you and your wife could become a powerful praying team?

∽ You possessed a secret for intensifying the love between you and your wife to such an extent that neither of you would, or could, imagine life apart—

developing a love that would become an example to family and friends of what marriage really should be.

The good news is that all of the above can become a reality in your marriage! Yet it begins when you learn how to ask the right questions and make a heart commitment to really listen as your wife shares her answers.

2

A MOMENT WASTED...A MARRIAGE WEAKENED

"What happened to the truck?"

It was one of those mornings filled with promise. The rising sun trailed its rays through the wispy clouds overhead. A night time spring rain had awakened the soil and in the rising sun the grasses along the roadside possessed an almost surreal green. I had just finished an early morning workout at a local health club and then visited over a cup of coffee with some men who frequently met with me there. To put it frankly, I was feeling great. "Never better!" I thought to myself as I exited the freeway and pulled to a stop at the intersection.

Wham! In a millisecond everything changed as a distracted young lady (just newly wedded, I discovered later) followed me off the exit and without slowing slammed into the rear of my automobile. I sat dazed for a moment after my car careened into the middle of the intersection and came to a stop. Then it occurred to me. While my injuries were minor, that might not be true of the person in the car behind me. Getting out of my car I ran back to the truck in which sat its weeping occupant. Assuring me that her injuries were also minor, other than the cut on her forehead, she allowed me to assist her into the front seat of my own automobile.

"I've got a mobile phone," I said, "so let's call and get you some help." She told me that her husband had gone to work early and she was on her way to a local hospital where she worked as a nurse. "Do you know your husband's number at work?" I asked, and then dialed the number as she slowly repeated it. With my mobile phone in its cradle, I was an audience to the conversation that followed.

After calling her husband off the shop floor, she sobbed out the story of the accident. "Buddy," I thought to myself, "this is your moment. Right now you have an incredible opportunity to speak love, understanding, and encouragement to your wife. Say the right thing and you will reveal the kind of love that captures the heart of any woman. Say the wrong thing and your marriage may not survive its first year. Don't blow it!"

With one question he blew it. It was a question, which spoke volumes about the young man, his value system, and the true love of his life.

"What happened to the truck?"

I cringed. The young lady wept. Then came the next question, equally as heartless:

"What do you want me to do?"

"Nothing, I guess," sighed the young wife, becoming irritated herself. Then she put her face in her hands and wept softly. "Let me give you my mother's number," she said. "She will help me."

Consider the incredible power of a question! With two questions, that insensitive husband had alienated his wife, driven her home to her mother for help and damaged his marriage...perhaps irreparably.

3

THE INCREDIBLE POWER OF A QUESTION

Jesus asked 183 different questions!

Think about the incredible power residing in a question. The young husband could have conveyed his concern by asking, "Are you all right?" This would have communicated to his wife that he valued her above all else. Or he could have asked, "Where are you?" indicating that he was on his way immediately to help her. But the questions he asked were about *him, his* truck, and *his* schedule, with not the least expression of concern for her. In fact, she was left with a problem much greater than a wrecked truck or a cut forehead.

Questions possess power. The sad departure of Adam and Eve from God's place for them in the Garden of Eden and the introduction of sin into the human race was precipitated with a question challenging God's authority. "Has God said," Satan asked of Eve, "you shall not eat of every tree of the garden?" Think of the consequences bound up in the response to that question!

Jesus frequently employed the power of a question. The four Gospels (Matthew, Mark, Luke, and John) record 297 questions asked by Christ of others. Given that there are multiple accounts of some events in more than one Gospel record, it is important to know that 183 of the questions He asked differed significantly in substance, time, or audience. The Master Teacher was keenly aware of the value in asking the right question.

It is not enough, however, simply to ask right questions. Of equal importance (and sometimes greater importance!) is an individual's willingness to really listen to the answer given. Nowhere is this more important than in family relationships.

4

LISTENING TO THE HEART OF YOUR WIFE

"If you won't listen...neither will God!"

Some years ago, my attention became riveted to a passage of scripture I had read many times before. This time it was different. I saw for the first time that the manner in which I listened to my wife directly impacted the manner in which God listened to me! Look at the verse.

"Likewise, you husbands, dwell with (your wives) according to knowledge, giving honor unto the wife as unto the weaker vessel (and by implication the vessel to be treasured), and as being heirs together of the grace of life; that your prayers not be hindered" (1 Peter 3:7).

This one verse actually speaks volumes about the importance of a husband listening to his wife! Think about your relationship with your wife as you contemplate what is said.

Listening is a prerequisite to knowing and understanding my wife!

"Dwell with your wife according to knowledge," writes Peter. What better way to know a person than to listen as they share their heart. That is

the first item on the agenda. Apply for a job, go to the doctor, request a credit card, or maybe even a loan on your house. There is a questionnaire to be completed. They want to know you! In fact, sometimes they want to know more than you think is justified!

Likewise, the way to know your wife is not only by asking questions but by giving your full, undivided attention as she responds. Nothing invites openness like the confidence that someone is giving their full attention to the answer. Nothing suppresses openness like the impression that you are speaking to someone who is distracted and actually disinterested.

Listening says to my wife, "You are important to me!"

"Give honor unto the wife," continues Peter. Listening communicates value to anyone—friend, associate, child, parent, and especially to your spouse! It's hard to convince someone you really care about them if you do not care much for what they are saying. Refusing to turn off the TV or radio, refusing to put down the paper, or to stop what you are doing and look someone squarely in the eye sends a message: *You are not the most important thing in my life— not even as important to me as the news, a favorite song or sitcom, or anything else for that matter.*

Marriages that will truly last are built upon the unique elements of love and communion. These are the marriages in which communication is a prized commodity. In fact, the couples who are most successful have regular, generally daily, times set aside specifically for the purpose of listening to one another. It is a way of saying, "I value you, and therefore I value what you have to say."

Listening reveals my understanding of God's grace.

"Treat your wife," says Peter, *"as a fellow heir of God's grace."* A refusal to listen to someone communicates the idea that you have an "edge" with God they do not possess. The old saying that, *"The ground is level at the foot of the cross,"* is true! A refusal to listen to the heart of another, especially your spouse, is an open denial of that truth. It indicates that you have a relationship with God which eliminates the necessity of listening to the one He as given you as your life's mate.

"My husband thinks he is God," said a frustrated wife to me one day. Then she continued by saying that he never sought her counsel on anything, and when it was offered, he actually scoffed at her. "I don't feel I'm part of the team," she said. "It's like he's the expert on everything and I'm just the little woman along for the ride. In fact, he pays more attention to our children than he does to me." This was a marriage already in deep trouble and being led into deeper trouble by a man who had little grasp of the grace of God!

If I won't listen...neither will God!

This is the part of the verse that captured my attention. *"We are to dwell with our wives according to knowledge, giving honor unto them as unto the weaker vessel, and as being heirs together of the grace of life; that our prayers not be hindered"!* In other words, my attentiveness to my spouse directly impacts God's attentiveness and response to me. That's a sobering thought!

In marriage, God says that a man and woman literally become *one flesh*. He looks upon us, not as two people who simply reside in the same house, but as a single unit. For me to ignore my wife's counsel, to refuse the attention she deserves, never asking the questions which open her heart to reveal the truth inside, is literally to ignore half of the reasoning and counsel God desires me to hear. Such deliberate neglect evokes a similar response from God. "Ignore the pleas of her heart," God is saying, "and I'll do the same to you."

A common Scriptural analogy of the church is that believers are "the bride of Christ." Similarly, the scripture repeatedly reminds us that "we reap what we sow." Peter is giving us an example of that very principle. "If you ignore your bride," he says to us, "you have little reason to expect that the Lord will treat you any differently!" Now that's worthy of your deepest consideration!

In reality, a question's ultimate power is directly related to your willingness to listen attentively to the answer. Let me tell you how I learned this principle.

5

A PERSONAL EXPERIENCE

"That moment marked one of the most significant turning paths in our marriage."

Every couple knows that it's possible to listen to "words" without actually hearing someone's "heart." True intimacy in the marriage relationship requires heart-to-heart communication. Proverbs 31 teaches that the husband of the "virtuous woman" was challenged to be a man of integrity because

"...his heart safely trusted in her." That is just one of the benefits of "heart-to-heart" communication.

So many distractions fill our lives that couples can easily drift miles apart, even while living under the same roof. Healthy communication is essential for a healthy marriage, but it requires the full attention of both parties. Dennis Rainey, popular radio host and founder of Family Life Today, once confessed that he was distracted with a television program while his wife was trying to talk with him. Finally, in exasperation she walked over to his chair, placed her hands on either side of his head, turned it toward her and pled, "Listen to me with your face." She wanted heart-to-heart communication.

For years, my wife Jeannie and I have enjoyed the happy, joyous privilege of heart to heart communication. Such communication requires honest effort. In addition to our daily morning time together (we also each have an individual quiet time), we have made a custom of taking at least one extended annual "get away" for our personal "R&R." During this time we assess our relationship, re-focus our priorities, and enjoy physical refreshment and exercise. We seek to hear from our Lord—and each other.

One year the Lord impressed me with ten questions I was to ask Jeannie. I desired to hear her heart so that as her husband I could properly respond. We found an idyllic setting at our favorite restaurant tucked away in the mountains near a beautiful lake as the perfect place for a wonderful, unhurried outdoor breakfast. The view was impressive, but I don't believe either of us was prepared for what God had in store for us!

Early that morning as we walked together from our lodge to the restaurant, I told Jeannie that I had ten questions I wanted to ask her. I encouraged her to answer each question openly and honestly and without any fear that I would become defensive. I promised that this was "her time" and determined to write down her answers. "Be careful how you answer," I promised, "because I will respond in love to each of your answers and with a determined effort to accommodate your desires."

That morning marked one of the most significant turning points in our marriage relationship. In fact, though we were already parents and grandparents, it was almost as if we were starting our marriage out all over again. Since then, I have made it a point to ask Jeannie these questions every year. As I have shared these questions in conferences, seminars, and retreats literally around the globe, I have been overwhelmed with the reports of the radical changes this simple practice has brought to marriages whatever the age or stage in life.

Before I share the questions, let me share *some words of caution*:

1) Be certain you make this a special, uninterrupted time with your wife. It will take planning and preparation on your part. That in itself will send a strong signal about your desire to hear her heart.

2) Do not ask her to write out her answers to these questions. Listen to her; ask her to explain more fully. *Then you write down her answers.*

3) Do not, I repeat, do not seek to defend, argue, rationalize, or otherwise explain your position on the issues she raises. You want to hear her heart. She may ask you questions at a later date (In fact, Jeannie now has a list of her own Ten Questions which she asks me every year!) *This is her moment* to tell you how she feels about these important issues.

4) As you come near the close, ask your wife if there are some questions she actually was wishing you would ask. Write them down, ask them, and record her answers.

5) In closing, tell your wife you want to study the answers she has given you. (You may want to review with her what you have written down.) Tell her your desire is to provide an affirmative response to each desire of her heart. After spending time alone

studying her responses, write out a pledge of your personal desire and determination to be the husband God wants you to be. Sign it, and give it to her. (A sample is included at the close of this book.)

Now...let's look at the questions!

6

10 QUESTIONS EVERY HUSBAND SHOULD ASK HIS WIFE EVERY YEAR

"You know those big game trophies hanging in the entry..."

1) What can I do to cause you to feel more loved and cherished?

Note that my emphasis here is on "feeling" not just "knowing." Perhaps you remember the story of the wife who endured fifty years with her non-communicative mate. Finally she asked him, "Do you love me?" "Look," her husband replied tersely, "I told you I loved you at the marriage altar, and if things change, I'll let you know!" Of course, his answer gave her little comfort!

Verbal affirmation of affection is sadly lacking in far too many marriages, but it is a practice that pays incredible dividends. While our entire family was living at home, each of us enjoyed telling the other family members, "I love you," every day. Even now, though most of our children live some distance from us, we find opportunity to frequently communicate of our love.

Causing someone to "feel" loved and cherished takes more than words! I was reminded of this need by Jeannie's response to my first question. We had been traveling a lot. Often we found ourselves in large groups of people with demands on one or the other of us. "I just want to know that *you know* I am along with you at those times," she confided. She wanted a visible recognition of our relationship.

Jeannie reminded me that in social settings, I often became so engaged in conversation with others that I left her to fend for herself. "I know you are trying to help people," she said, "but I still want you to pull out my chair at the dinner table." Ouch! (I was beginning to wonder if I should ask the other nine questions). Jeannie wasn't selfishly craving attention; she simply desired my acknowledgement and respect for her presence as my wife. Feeling respected by your mate has a great deal to do with feeling loved.

I am convinced that growth and intimacy in marriage will take place only when each partner is doing everything necessary to insure that the other feels genuinely loved and cherished. What others may say or do to us is always tempered by our sense of whether they truly love us. Genuine love always expresses respect.

2. How can I best demonstrate my appreciation for you, your ideas, and your role as my wife?

A little background will be helpful here. A few days earlier while preparing to lead a seminar on prayer, I read Peter's admonition which we have already examined, the admonition for husbands to dwell with their wives, *"According to knowledge, giving honor unto the wife as unto the weaker vessel,*

and as being heirs to together of the grace of life;
that your prayers be not hindered" (1 Peter: 3:7).
Moreover, I had made a mental note to remind the
husbands in the audience that the effectiveness of
their prayers was directly related to the manner in
which they responded to the needs of their wives.
Now I was attempting to follow my own (and the
Lord's) counsel.

My wife, by the way, is uniquely gifted as a
ladies' Bible teacher. Using that gift is one of her
greatest joys. But I had sent signals that somehow I
felt her gifts were inferior to mine. Jeannie reminded
me of a recent occasion when I had urged her to
come with me as I fulfilled a speaking engagement.
She had reminded me, "Going with you would
conflict with the ladies Bible class I teach each

week." "That's all right." I had responded off-handedly, "Just get somebody to fill in for you!"

With that remark, I had conveyed the impression that a responsibility she had prayerfully assumed was insignificant in comparison to what I was doing. I now realized that I was asking her to give up an assignment for which she had prepared both intellectually and spiritually just so I would not have to drive alone across town to deliver a message she had heard several times. She had assured me that she was willing to do so if I felt it was important. It was obvious that I wanted her to sacrifice her important commitment merely for my own convenience.

Recently I was counseling a couple struggling with this same issue. When I asked the wife to describe what was troubling her, she said, "My husband always speaks of me as his 'better half', but in reality I feel that my ideas, concerns, and input amount to far less than a half of our relationship. I would just like to know if he really means what he says."

3. What can I do to assure you that I hear and understand your heart's desires?

Jeannie's answer to this question was simple, and it brought a sense of relief to my heart. "The very thing that you are doing right now tells me that you really want to know my heart," she said. Discovering the "heart desires" of our spouse takes time, attention, focus, and above all, a determination to talk about a matter until both understand one another.

As a pastor I have had the opportunity to counsel many married couples. Over the years, I have discovered that some couples have very little understanding of one another. In fact, many appear to build high walls in their heart to keep their spouse from really getting to the truth. Sometimes people build walls because they would be ashamed for their spouse to discover the truth. At other times, they are hiding some cherished thought which they feel their mate would not value highly.

My wife was encouraged by the fact that I had gone to great lengths to develop these questions and then waited for an appropriate time to ask them. I had stayed with each issue until assured I had the "whole truth." Then I had covenanted with her to respond in the affirmative to each of her answers (without argument or self defense!). All this spoke volumes to her heart.

4. What can I do to make you feel absolutely secure?

Here, I was addressing the issue of security on several different levels: physical, emotional, and relational. Again my wife's answer took me off guard. As I have mentioned above, I had been traveling a great deal. Sometimes Jeannie would be at home alone over a period of several days. Since we had other family members nearby however, I was surprised by her answer: "Install an alarm system in the house!"

This kind of protection had crossed my mind before, but I just hadn't gotten around to it. My immediate thought was to remind her that our neighborhood had experienced virtually no problems with security. I could explain just how securely our house was positioned at the end of our cul-de-sac. Or, I could give her the old, "Unless the Lord keep the house" lecture.

But I had promised to hear my wife's heart and to respond positively. So I listened. She explained her reasons: our dog had died, the bedroom was at the far end of the house, and more. As I listened, I realized that I needed to act. In less than a week the alarm system was installed. I wanted Jeannie to see that I really meant business when I said I would to respond positively to her heart's concerns.

Speaking with other people, I have discovered that some individuals place emotional, moral, or marital security above the physical. Our Adversary has many ways of breaking and entering our homes. It is imperative to stand on guard and to take whatever action is necessary to bring a sense of security into our homes.

I recall one wife saying to me that, as her husband watched TV, she watched her husband watch TV. Disconcerted because of what seemed to grab his attention as he surfed the channels with the "power bar," she began to develop great insecurities about his moral integrity and their own relationship. On other occasions I have listened to a husband or a wife voice concern over relationships which threatened the stability of their home. Perhaps it was a job which repeatedly placed their mate in a compromising situation. In each instance, the security of the home was placed at risk.

If not addressed appropriately, feelings of insecurity or lack of confidence will hover over a home like an oppressive cloud. With their differing gifts and responsibilities, a husband or wife will often sense a threat to which the other may be totally oblivious. For a secure home, both husband and wife must hear each other out on these issues, and they must respond with immediate and positive action.

5. *What can I do to insure that you have confidence and joy in our future direction?*

When I first asked these ten questions, we were in the beginning throes of the "empty nest" syndrome. With our children either married or in college, the pattern of our lives began to change. I admit that we were enjoying some things about the change (Someone once said that life begins when the dog dies and the children leave home!). What were we going to do with our newfound freedom? What were God's plans for the rest of our lives?

Now, after sharing these ten questions with groups of all ages, I have concluded that this one question should be asked often and reviewed at every stage of marriage. Notice that the question concerns "our" future direction. This question was my way of reminding Jeannie that whatever course God chose for our lives, we would obey together. Too many couples have accepted the fantasy that marriage allows the husband and wife the privilege of living together while each does his or her "own thing." Husbands in particular tend to move away from the heart of their wives by "announcing" their plans for the future and simply assuming that what brings joy to the husband will also bring joy to the wife.

The purpose of this important question was to say to my wife, "Whatever we do must be something endorsed by your heart as well as mine." I find that some men are threatened by this approach because they feel that they are surrendering authority or leadership. In reality the very opposite is true. This question only encourages confidence and trust. It shows you want to be a leader like Jesus, a "servant leader," one who seeks the best interest of those you serve in love.

In the end, my wife's answer to this question surprised me by its simplicity. As a matter of fact, Jeannie and I set aside a specific time during the next few days to plan our "future direction" together. Our discussion excited us about the possibility of bringing to reality some things we had only dreamed of doing.

6. What attribute or practice would you like to see me develop or improve? Is there something in my life you would prefer I eliminated?

You are acquainted, I'm sure, with people who mistakenly believe they have reached an age or a stage in life beyond which no significant decisions will ever be made. They consider that their best years, the years of greatest effectiveness, are behind them. Are we talking "old" here? Not necessarily! I've met folks in their twenties who have adopted this opinion of themselves and their possibilities.

I asked Jeannie this question because the opportunities for a more effective life are *always* present. Currently, one of my most admired mentors is enjoying amazing effectiveness at the age of ninety-seven! Thousands visit his Internet web site on a regular basis. He has a speaking schedule which would exhaust many. He is currently working on three books. He consults with two of the world's largest mission enterprises; and to top it off he enjoys the kind of vigorous health (like Caleb's) always associated with having a sense of "purpose." His secret? An eager approach to new ideas and a readiness to change.

I learned from my friend that, at the age of fifty-five, he completed a Ph.D. in Classical Rhetoric in order to possess the credentials for founding his dream, a seminary which has trained thousands of students. "I want to be like that man!" I said to my wife and we promptly "adopted" him. The greatest lesson he has taught me is that our utility (our usefulness to the Lord) can actually increase every day of our lives. In other words, our latest years can be our greatest years!

My wife had a ready response my question. She reminded me that while the children had been at home, I faithfully practiced a discipline which meant more to her than I imagined. We had developed the practice of rising early, having our own personal "quiet time" with the Lord, then meeting together for thirty minutes of unhurried conversation followed by a family breakfast. Now that the children were gone and with no push to get them to school, we still had our individual quiet times, but following that, I often scheduled early morning appointments.

"I miss our time together, "she said, "and the anchor of our breakfast time each morning." Her request for us to resume that former practice was a sobering reminder that I was neglecting a mutually beneficial formula of togetherness for our marriage. Her request would require an adjustment to my practice of early morning appointments. But I had said, "No arguments!" Once again, that time together has become an anchor for us as we begin each day.

7. What attribute would you most like to develop in yourself? How may I help you in the best possible way?

Each of us generally has a ready answer to this question. My wife, in fact, was not at a loss for an answer herself. But the vital issue centered on the second part of the question: How may I help you in the best possible way?

Of course, my tendency is to think that all problems can be solved with words. If soft words don't help, use hard ones. If logic doesn't work, use the sarcastic and barbed approach. If few words don't get the job done, use many. If an appeal doesn't work, use forceful language. You get the picture!

But now it was my wife's turn to help *me* get the picture. She opened her heart about a part of her life in which she was seeking improvement. She told me how God was speaking to her heart. She shared that God's Spirit had long ago convicted her about a specific issue, and she was eager for change. Unfortunately, my past attempts to use "words" had only brought resentment and an eagerness to defend herself. It had only made matters worse.

Her openness enabled me to discover how I could be a true partner with my wife. I began to see how I could encourage her as she sought to obey God's conviction. Simply by asking this question and by listening intently to her answer, I showed my desire to fulfill that helpful role. I was saying, "I'm on your side but as a cheerleader, not a hard driving coach!" That new approach has made all the difference…in both our lives.

8. Is there some accomplishment in my life that would bring joy to your heart?

I thought Jeannie would say, "You know those big game trophies hanging in our entry? I want more, many more of them. Come on Safari Man! I want a house full of those beauties!" I'm still stunned and a little confused as to why she didn't respond in that fashion!

She did share with me, however, that she felt very strongly about my completing a specific project that I had been fussing over for some period of time. Then she shared something else, her reason for wanting me to complete the project and confidence that the Lord would use it. She challenged me to finish it within the year, reminding me that once it was completed, I would be free in my own heart to turn my attention to other issues. Since I had promised, "No argument!" I accepted the challenge, and soon it was off to the publisher.

What most encouraged me was the fact that she also believed there was much more for us to accomplish together in the balance of our lives. She needed to hear that I also felt as she did and that I was willing to accept the challenge. If I had responded negatively she would have wondered, "Just what will we do with the balance of our lives? Will those years be filled with uncompleted tasks and un-reached goals?"

The Bible is filled with examples of men and women who proved that life is not over until it's over. Remember Caleb, Joshua's partner, one of only two men in Israel's original army who were allowed the privilege of entering the Promised Land? Caleb's secret of strength, the driving force accompanying him through forty years in the wilderness, was the simple fact that God had promised him a specific piece of real estate and the ability to gain it. At the age of eighty-five, he asserted his claim, "Now therefore give me this mountain!" His goal kept him going!

After years of marriage counseling, I have come to believe that few things bring distress to a wife like the failure of her husband to have clear, positive objectives for the future. And nothing so encourages a man as the privilege of accomplishment!

9. What would indicate to you my desire to be more like Christ?

With this question I wanted to communicate my eagerness, above all, to be like my Lord. When I perform marriages I remind couples that there is no safer place for them in the heart of their spouse than second place, as long as Christ is in first place. The best way for a man to love his wife and children is for him to love Christ above all.

Jeannie needed to see indications of my desire to be Christ-like. There needed to be evidences of growth in my relationship to Him and the sense that I was actually being conformed to His image. But what are those signs? She told me that there were four visible indicators which spoke volumes to her about the state of my spiritual life.

Prayer, or communion with the Father, was one of those indicators. Not just occasional prayer. Prayer as a matter of etiquette at mealtimes, or prayer when "called upon", but a life of prayer. Jeannie told me that one of her favorite mental pictures is one where I am in the chair where I spend time with the Lord, taking the needs of our family before the Him. "I'd like to see more of that," she said.

Genuine interest in the Word of God (a hunger and thirst for the Bible and an eagerness to apply its principles) is another sign. I have often said that the legacy I want to leave my children is the knowledge that God is faithful to those who live by His Word. But how would a man know what it is to live by the Word if he didn't spend time in it? Jeannie reminded me that she was always encouraged when she saw that the Bible was more to me than a resource for speaking engagements.

Another evidence of a heart for God is *a sensitivity to sin and promptness in putting it aside the moment God's Spirit brings conviction.* Hanging on to bad habits, attitudes, friends, or practices are the first clues that a man is not practicing the Lordship of Christ. A willingness to confess and repent of sin, on the other hand, is a sign of spiritual vitality.

A life marked by the fruit of the Spirit is another outward sign of Christ-likeness. Fruit is the outward expression of one's inward nature. As you surrender to Christ's Lordship, the Holy Spirit will produce love, joy, peace, longsuffering, gentleness, goodness, faith, meekness, and temperance. This is a "cluster." Where you find anyone of them, you will find them all.

Your marriage partner deserves the joy of knowing that, above all else, you want to be like Jesus. Nothing will bring greater confidence than to know that Christ is *running the show*...in your heart and in your home.

10. What mutual goal(s) would you like to see us accomplish together?

Here is the message I wanted to send with this question: This marriage is not about me; it is about us. I believe God put us together for a reason, and I want to be sure we are accomplishing all He intended.

Jeannie and I view marriage as a life "together." That was not the issue here. My concern was that we maximize the contribution we can make during our brief time on this earth. I already had some ideas regarding specific things we might accomplish together, ministries we might perform. *But were these on her heart as well?*

You cannot imagine the manner in which answering this question will open the door of "partnership" in marriage. You will began to "check up" on the progress you are making, holding one another accountable, and rejoicing together when specific objectives are reached. As we discussed our goals for our own relationship, our family, and the ministry opportunities God had placed at our disposal, I discovered that, in some areas, *my wife's vision far exceeded my own*. In other areas mine was a challenge to her. We were able to hammer out some clear sense of what we wanted to see accomplished at specific periods in our lives, should God allow it. We then approached life together with a new sense of excitement and purpose.

7

A PLEDGE

"...And then I signed my name."

Are you willing to ask these "Ten Questions" openly, without argument, and with a mind to respond positively? Following our time together, I wrote down on a single page my wife's responses to these questions. At the bottom of that page I wrote the following words, and then signed my name:

"Believing that the Lord has spoken to my heart through you; desiring to answer in the

affirmative to each request; and realizing that the answer to many of them will require specific measurable action on my part, I indicate to you, by this signature, my determination to fulfill these desires of your heart."

Signed _____

Date _____

8

A FINAL WORD TO HUSBANDS

"God will honor your prayer as you honor your wife."

"These questions don't work!" a young husband said to me one day. "I wrote them out on a piece of paper, handed the paper to my wife with the request that she fill it out at her convenience. Not only has she not completed what I asked her to do, she actually seems angry at me!" *And for good reason,* I thought to myself.

What is the key? Is it the questions? Your willingness to set aside a special time to ask them? Your determination to listen to your wife's heart? Writing down her answers? Contemplating them, and then pledging your determination to respond in the affirmative to each of her desires?

Frankly, I believe the answer is found in all the above. It is with an overwhelming sense of confidence that I pass them along to you, assured that God will honor your prayers as you honor your wife. So set aside the time, make the date. Your life and your marriage will never be the same.

LOOK FOR...

10 Questions
Every Wife Should Ask
Her Husband Every Year

By Jeannie Elliff

Questions which will help you discover the
"true Heart" of your mate.

AND...

10 Questions
Parents Should Ask
Their Children

By Tom and Jeannie Elliff

What you don't know can hurt you and devastate your child.

OTHER BOOKS TO READ

Letters to Lovers

(Published by Broadman and Holman)

By Tom and Jeannie Elliff

Wisdom for every season of your marriage.

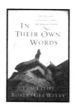

In Their Own Words

(Published by Broadman and Holman)

By Tom Elliff and Robert Gee WItty

Exciting, life-changing personal testimonies.

Unbreakable:
The Seven Pillars of a Kingdom Family

(Published by Broadman and Holman)

By Tom Elliff

How to build your life and family on the
indestructible principles of God.

A Passion For Prayer

(Published by Crossway)

By Tom Elliff

How to experience deeper intimacy with God through prayer.

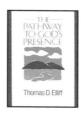

The Pathway to God's Presence

(Published by Broadman and Holman)

By Tom Elliff

Learning to walk hand in hand with God.

American on the Edge

(Published by NCM Press)

By Tom Elliff

What to do when it's later than you think.

Praying For Others

(Published by Broadman and Holman)

By Tom Elliff

Basic instructions for the intercessor.

To purchase these and other books by Tom Elliff, contact your local Christian Book Store, or write to:

Living in the Word Publications

P.O. Box 891474

Oklahoma City, Oklahoma 73189-1474

Phone: 1-405-732-1300